NOTHING TAKES ALL

NOTHING TAKES ALL

ANINDYA GHOSH

PARTRIDGE

ISBN: Hardcover 978-1-5437-0890-5
Softcover 978-1-5437-0892-9
eBook 978-1-5437-0891-2

Images by Rituparna Ghosh

Print information available on the last page.

To order additional copies of this book, contact
Partridge India
000 800 919 0634 (Call Free)
+91 000 80091 90634 (Outside India)
orders.india@partridgepublishing.com

www.partridgepublishing.com/india

Contents

Dedicated to

Amma and Maa

Foreword

Poetry. The gurus have decreed, is a form of delirium; an opiate to counter the pain of living; a prayer and incantation; a nostalgia for a world of lost innocence; a call to change the hearts & minds of people gone mad and much more.

In trying to hack the trees in a chaotic world, Ghosh bloodies his own fingers and in trying to touch the absolute, frequently puts his mind dangerously out of gear. He does not visit hell like Dante, rather he chooses to go there like a Greek chorus. He delineates a calligraphy of bone and ash. In his ode to rooted reality, unseen, Ghosh powerfully closes in on spiritual India with digital eyes.

These are poems, complex, abstract and esoteric, powered clearly with emotional confidence, reaffirming the simple fact that human sensibilities can only expand when we open our eyes, mind, heart and imagination to events unfolding around us, with honesty, passion and purpose.

By

Monojit Lahiri

Monojit Lahiri is a Kolkata-based communication practitioner specialising in Cinema, Advertising & Popular culture. He has journeyed this space for over 4 decades.He consciously invests his material with doses of entertainment, engagement and relevance, and has zero interest in changing the world!

Nu

Let us not talk any more,
Nor sing, nor hum,
Not trying through signs,
Nor Coptic words, written or told;
Let us just raise the magical
Peristeria blooming from our ears,
Which will stop all the noises
Reaching.
Let's take a walk into the
Ten dimensions of our being—

To the terrain of sun-beaten biomes
Where the Joshua trees line.
The wind-scoured mesas and mountains.
Mesquites and saguaros
Along the dried-up playas.
Eyes of coyotes look at the blood moon,
And the star lore whispers.

Or a walk to the giant deciduous Semul
in the tropics, the dense foliage
Of the red Shalmali flowers
And vipers dripping venom from the
Kalpavriksh.
A fire of sacrifice in the middle of darkness,
Leopards waiting and thirsting in ambush,
While the silent hymns
Chant the surreal.

Let us return to our
Primitive thoughtlessness,
The cold and colourless
Metacosm of nothing.
An all-pervading water of creation
Which is yet to be.
No waves, no weasels.
No bubbles, no shapes.
A depth of an empty I-ness,
Phenomena and the noumena.

Aghora

Born of darkness, I am.
A slithery, worm-infested hollow way,
Strewn with carcasses
And decayed bodies of plants.
It has no direction, no shape,
Scattered—enshrouding me
Like a mother's breasts, hands,
Cradling me with lullabies
And slowly penetrating
With a wriggling lunacy,
Scratching and scrawling on my mind,
Spreading roots,
Stemming blue veins with sharp teeth and claws,
Carrying stains of blood
From sins of my earlier birth.

The hair looms in the still of night
And crawls under my bed
In a green light of doom: heresy.
Mayan flowers bloom on the walls.
My whole body, a miasma of dark spells.
Windows screech and shudder,
And the sky rushes to a darker hole,
Where the garden of souls
Writhes in a wuthering cry.
I have not become a man, a woman,
Or any of the in-betweeners—
Only a river of blood
Flowing over heaps of skulls and bones
Across a valley,
A valley of fireflies.

On Seeing Nostalgia

Remaining home.
The hallway has grown jungles—
Tropical trees with fleshy leaves,
Moist darkness, blooming hibiscus,
Choking heat of dimness, and the sweat.
Closed windows of arabesque panes.
Far end, where the giant clock lies, crashed.
Bevelled glasses, shattered;
The serpentine hands, loosened;
And the burl overlays, rotting, dampened.
Only a single strike every hour—
Filling the time, passed.

On the dining lies the body of a man.
Weathered sediments of mud and carcasses
Half nude.
Some shamanic rites had just been finished.
Burnt coals and wisps of fumes from parts of the body,
Pagan drawings on thighs and hands.
A circle of black ice melts on the chest.
Drops of water falling from an unknown sky,
On the eyes, cheeks—
The soul is made to cry.
Locks of marigold breeze the banisters.

Corridor to the kitchen and other rooms.
Walls frescoed with the image of Indra, the king of gods,
Cursed to have a thousand vaginas on his body.
Empty rooms, beds from the rooms all
Stacked up in the kitchen.
Linens and pyjamas with stains of turmeric and other spices,
Acidic stink of dead fishes, green frogs slurping and looking,
Wooden cabinets filled with blood-soiled poultices
And in the attic, a huge fire burns, thick brown smoke,
Smutting the walls, a red knot of threads: chants,
Feng shui dolls descending from the ceiling—
Many happy Buddhas,
And the three Chinese stars,
Fuk, Luk, Shou.
Fuk, Luk, Shou.

Will Distances

Keep your hands beside mine?
How different they look—
My hands, fair, showing the blue veins
Running like estuaries in
The wetlands of Ob.
And yours so dark and fleshy,
With the white nails
Capturing all the light
There is, and reflections
From the far Kibo
Between them.

When the ancient sea rises
And Mother Earth
Goes for weaving beads in
The deep oceans robed
In blood blankets and
Necklaces from Xhosa,
The trees take long strides,
A sound of caresses blow
Through them, and
In a half sun and half night,
A herd of zebras copulate.
That sky comes to us
In oblivion and falls on our hands.

We spread roots and build inside—
Room, a window to view;
Our worlds of perception,
Of love, ancestries, and legends;
Where exploits are explorations,
Ancient rituals are heresies,
And blackness is filth:
A monument of lies,
A suppression of history.
So let us enter the forests of Biloko.
There our hands entwine,
In blood, in wrinkles, in despair;
The dashiki dances in moonlight, fading drums.
A whole saga of a river in your lips,
A vast wilderness of desert in my eyes.

The Zen in Death

Then the dead body arrives at the corridor,
Floating, surrounded by candles.
Nobody can touch it;
The face, washed with a soft light,
As if sleeping deeply, dreaming.
A pinch of a smile—or not.
Gongs in the German clock, the abelia blooms.
I am dragged to see her dead face—
How she shuts her eyes,
How she does not breathe any more,
How she will never say a thing to me.
Does it feel different?
Why do I have to see?
Have I not known from times
And times and times before, I have killed her?
In love, in despair, in silences.
What did she touch last?
Not my hands, nor my eyes,
Not the little flower dry between the books.
Or was it the silicone mask at the hospital bed,
The vinyl pillows, swabbed and sterilised?

Hunger thralls; I put on my mittens
To enter the refrigerator.
All that's there are some fish bones
and a lazing cat whose tongue
Now has been cut off.
She bleeds with her eyes open.

Gory, looming eyes, brown and cruel.
Further up, a river has frozen; I stand on
the bank and shout your name
Again and again and again.
Only the birches and the elms echo.
Somewhere, a phone rings.
And though no one picks up, a
conversation starts, in whispers.
A girl's voice weeping and the sound of an elevator
Going up and down, up and down, up and down.
A distant window lit up in a dark building,
A mirror ringing as well in a vacant office space.
Too many tables, too many tables,
Papers, heaps, cabinets, computers.
The mirror goes on ringing,
Shakes violently, I—the reflection.
I—the reflection, hazy, shaking, distorted.

Istanbul Diaries 1

The first night is an illusion. I enter the *marifat*, embellished in a Turkish *cubbe* and golden nose rings. My flight of ecstasy in water, in air, in fire, with the flock of seagulls which encircle the crown of the blue mosque in mystic serendipity. The tears of the angels fall into the Marmara Sea, and the sea rumbles. The black water shifts, shimmers in darkness, and my eyes come back to me, like an evening bird. I have no beginning, no end. The stoned pavements lead me to the ways of many forests, with chandeliers hanging from trees, smoke from an unknown fire, and burnt meat of deer, all melting in the air. Red walls of history lost in you, the stretch of your longing, the pastures of desire, and the bold calligraphy of love and desperation.

Death is just this fragrance in the garden. I hear your whispers from the dreams; you have gone away from yourself. Maybe in search of the moon, with shining armour. Once the sword is out of its scabbard, the moon will shine in brilliance. Wings in blood, I play the *rubab* from under the water; the face of the dervish is illumined. He is happy in his hands, in his steps, in his ether, in the connect. One, two, three, and four. The four stars fall from the sky, slowly, on to the palms of my hands. I close them. Here is eternity, and I give this to you, a little from my vastness.

Istanbul Diaries 2

Day breaks in *ezan*. The muezzin's voice falls in the room like scattered pearls; some light stirs inside. I tiptoe to the red curtains, a chiaroscuro of love and fear, the fear of *kashf*, the unveiling of the Supreme. Do I see? Here the mountains rise from the black waters, floating red clouds of revelations. I writhe in agony for the struggle of the search; such a knowing fills the heart, overwhelming. Why has this thunder not struck me before?

All the pigeons fly with their wings on fire; I am not the same self who walked this path. Hammam and other quarters of cleaning. If I watch the rose in the garden, it will instantly bloom for me; the fountain will dance, and the sky will pour light. Oh my beloved! You have opened all the doors for me; from darkness to bliss I walk. The more I walk, the more paths unfold. You are everywhere—following me, leading me, and walking by my side.

This city I step in, blooms the tree of heaven. From each corner plays the saz, the *ilahi* throngs in the air, the dervish miraculously appears on the sidewalks and the troubadours' songs whisper love in the air. Have I never been born in this paradise? Mevlana lies far off in the hills, peacefully sleeping in his tomb. I sit on the banks of Marmara with a bouquet of roses and burn each petal to ashes in the moonlight. I offer myself to him. Let me fade into non-existence, while the nightingale calls from the mulberry tree and the spirit of my poet drinks wine—the blood, the soul.

Istanbul Diaries 3

Leaving you was not easy. A square of moonlight where the fountain changes its colours. Red, blue, green, purple. I keep running further and further away from things, shining. I: white walls, the diptych tiles' stares. A blue room in suicide. These tulips, the Seljuk patterns, the turquoise arabesques say something, hypnotic. A graveyard with blood-red roses, the inebriation of *bakhoor*, a *mukhallat* in *oudd*, the hands I have. The sensations of the gyrating body of the belly dancer. Her pouring breasts and dominations. The dark water of the Bosporus shimmers.

Where have I reached this place in smoke and muffled voices? The *sisha*, the old market, the tavern a room of dead men silently smoking. The visuals run, the empire shattered, dreams of kingdoms, icons and power, the sultanate. Here the bus starts. Dark lanes with narrow byroads. Let us have the last tea, in saffron, a tea in guilt and defeats, trying and still failing. At the turning, the effendi stands, an old man standing for ages at his stall below a tree older than him. With a leaf, memories fall, showers of evening sadness, maybe a hammam bath, maybe the museum walk, maybe a journey to another ruin on Mount Nemrut. All of which you had for me in shadows and promises, Istanbul, you know. Au revoir.

Dreams and May Not Be

There is so much to say
when we are not talking to each other.
The heart is pounding
as if in an interstellar space—
of stars and galaxies,
of meteors and planetoids.
A silence of under water
A cosmic oozing.

These are drops of blood
smeared on my chest.
You squiggle to form figures, vague words on it;
they don't make sense to me.
Your touch, the blood.
I want to jump
from planes of one phenomenon
to another of null, of a void.
A wave is lost.
Bandage over my ears, eyes, and neck.
I sit in ovulation, with a ruptured heart
and more damage to fertilise it.

The dog barks outside in the night
and keeps following me
through tunnel after tunnel in the dream.
Your big house of agony.
Walking in your sleep, you
take it gently.
Near the garden where the carousel stands,
the greenhorns have turned me into a shrub—
they know how to.
They have just uprooted my left ventricle,
dripping, raw—it tasted fine.

Love, yet Love

- Do you love me?

- I don't know this place. It's an attic sort of room, small window at the ceiling's edge, beams of diffused light. I hang face down, belts tied to my arms and limbs, naked. Some roots descend from my chest towards the ground yet not touching it. It is a pain as they branch and branch further and become heavy.

- Do you love me?

- Meadows of green rain. An underlying matrix of circuits. Trees move digitally, bushes in a line. Designated paths. I am made to stand like a pawn, still. Hands stretched out. Holding a sea bass in one, and in the other, the head of a reindeer. Many bridges explode one by one at a distance. Crystal fountains dance in an oblivion, a symphony.

- Do you want me?

- In my memories of walking, cities. *Jour de fête*. Colours in flags, carousels, kids shouting, and aromas of street foods. Suddenly, an explosionof flying trucks, wagons. Something spreads in the air, colourless. The faces and lips all around turning blue, children's mouths foam with green bubbles, red eyes. Asphyxiated. Blood dances in me. I evaporate.

- [Silence.]

- I do, love do. Don't be silent. Let us start. The universe explodes; galaxies break. Everything is moving away from everything. There is though gravity, though love, though our hands, our kisses, touches, and progenies. Everything shifts away in the interstellar darkness, and we . . . and we . . .

Rooms Are Blue, Falling

The versatile pain, and lethal
Blue beads of dangling sadness
Night comes in an envelope
Encrypted address
City stops dead at the signal
Psychedelics of red, green, amber
Amber, green, red, and red, green—darkness.

I am my bag
Razors, underwear, powerbanks, condoms
Chargers, fingertips, sun guards, lip guards
Thought guards, selfies, selfie lenses and sticks
Dip your hands in my pants
Cigarettes and an ancient matchbox
Pictures of a damsel, her lips
On the other side
A warship with green corpses.

Let us
Coitus of our legs
Hairs and bruises, despaired
Walking dreams, pleasures
Seas
Visions floating—willows, a red church
Stray books lying amongst the bluebells
Heaped dead bodies, a women doing laundry
Yet far, I am quiet in the rain

Standing at the sorrows of a bridge
Drenched
In fungi of memories, of a deserted home
Oblong lights, half-lit windows
Where in lonely rooms, all have been packed, yet not taken
Only a tiny weebill, lost, stares around
In emptiness, in time
Locked
Forever and after.

Come to the Frozen

Twilights murmur.
Some are but quieter,
like your poems.
Walking boulevards in silence
and fear,
turning to the secret side
of the chateaux.
Unknown, untrodden—dusks
of paths scattered with gillyflowers.
I sink in you with a room.
Glistening lips from the midnightly eerie
church bell gongs.
Losing one by one
my hands, legs, face
—the darkness of your lagoon.
Oblong cemeteries, cliffs in blue
brutal rivers, the monsters of your garden
dig me out from blood.
Guilts of my ancestral heresy—
my wars.
Defeats, complexities.
Our days faze:
a theft in soul—
cellars of hiding and holding ourselves.
Blackouts.
Blackouts.

Inside we are of each other; we love
with splintered heads of children,
with women wronged and killed,
with looted and destroyed monuments,
with falcons of war and more wars,
with us,
with us.
We fuck.

Calcutta, Twilights

1.

Jungle of violence
Death images
Pleurisy of thoughts
Still keep me in my knowing
Love, can you
Can you love?

2.

All shattering a joy
Dark sunglasses to dear sorrows
Pick me up from my dailyness
Love, you can, only you . . .

To My Daughter

Boundaries are oceans
All walls fall like waves
There's always an other side
Let Shangri-La be for your
Calm under the wheel of time
And wait for your tree
Only a few connect.

Collapse

I inhaled the sun,
and the bridge collapsed in a tremor.
Cars on it were thrown to the sky,
where they entered the clouds in lightning;
ones walking floated on the sphere of doom.
Houses around turned off their lights,
and an evening descended, gorging,
where I continued standing on the collapse,
looking at a far window of my decadence.

Pillars kept crashing in disarray
I started eating doubts and suspicions.
Dust and blast blackened my face,
and one of my eyes became of stone.
Everybody flying looked, everybody flying looked.
And at once I receded into vagaries of darkness;
I felt worms inside me, crawling fat worms.
I looked at the beautiful bigness of destruction
and relished how people die,
inside, outside, in nothingness, and in perpetuity.

Sights of devastation are of abstractness and delight.
I know I still exist when others fall.
I know that goodness is an evil which
should surely be trampled.
A bluish-green light plays on the massacre;
a quarry of living, who had their hands
in the hands of the dead,
stand in a never-ending line of grief.

Lives in grief will learn to follow, shivering.
Lives in resentment will not look at flowers, remorseful.
There will be no magic for them, a caustic grimness.
Or they won't live at all, bodies in paraffin.
A ruthless silence, spaced-out demolition,
and a tormenting wind remain.

And I

travel to the next targets of my explosion,
another bridge, a train, a church, or a busy road in a festival.
Endless romances.

In Me Jungle, Cold You

Sun, your tears
Green growths of vastness
Upturned sky
Sometimes a rendezvous
your little hands
your little hands.

Lights strike in cold
That island, a prayer
Bells chime
And blueness descends
your whispering eyes
your rendezvous eyes.

Some paths through a castle
Hollowness—a time
Dissections and clotted blood
Kingdom of loneliness
you and your you
me and your you.

Leaving or We, the Lonely Plays

Weeds are mine, and you keep the overcoat.
Rashes came on your shoulder, remember.
It was tuna or the new cheddar.
Mashed mornings or maybe my last silences;
Moons double when we two stand lonely in the veranda.
Might try the broken shades, myopic darkness's.

Open ajar the suitcase, arrange again; everything must fit.
Gloves, cardigans, the blue suit,
distances, honey, and fried minds.
Windows of nights, days—days' nights.
Candles, superstitions, and the blue
weeds under the canal water.
Before you say anything, always the doorbell rings.
Throttle me in silence when I stare
at you, my eyes not closed.

You used the photo editor to remove my red eyes;
The picture is looking good now.
Maybe a little bit of shadow would talk more.
Or increase the clarity, curtail the sides,
Frame the stillness, eyelessness.
The ghosts of our smiles, the pretence of our faces.
The frame will stand near your timepiece,
And the timepiece will tick.

Suicide on the Top of a Tree

I have sleep in me,
A sleep like a thorned laurel pressed over my head,
And trickles of blood saturating my forehead, eyes,
Dropping across the corners of my nose,
Embalming the sinisterness.

Still, the eyes stay open, in convolutions of thoughts,
And the python moves in all its black-and-yellowish girdles,
A slow and poisonous move, shimmering,
And shaking my body with an obscurity.

While the moon breaks rapturously,
And the splinters travel through the sky in whiteness,
Leaving the marks of their trajectories,
And fall on my eyes like cold and pointed swords.

Night turns the bed linens into a starry beach,
Where a dilapidated house shores
all the silences and uncanny.
I know that your golden legs are now
spread for a different warmth,
But my darkness fluttering in the sea breeze,
And the handfuls of sand slipping away in wilderness,
Are nothing but you,
And will be always.

The Sky, The Sky

Vaguely raining, in tenderness and half-light,
As if the last careful touches of water to the canvas,
And a lonesome walk through a path in the painting.

Faces drop from the slippery sky and
become a part of my wetness;
Darkness gives a delusion of light, a
glowing fever of nostalgia.
Roads dazzle in succulence, a moveable feast of the evening.
Jealousy flows in green tunnels of night,
Perhaps closed shops, windows open in longings and distant thoughts.

I am going to kill a kangaroo tonight.
Passing a long mirror and a bridge which sways over a bridge and another,
Fold me in twilight and keep me beside the fountain.
You are only wearing a tree which
bloomed in glorious fuchsias,
Trying to unfold my letter, and please don't.
I lost my blue pen in the swim of the letters,
Yet to finish and say my last words, the last words will be......

To Mrs Sen

Scurried flowers on the bed.
Tattered dandelions.
And a dark chair
In the shadows,
Cold and illumined.

A knock on the closed doors.
An urge to open at once.
A silence brewing in the room.
And then departing voices,
Departing voices
Far gone and never to return.

Whose eyes were the illness.
A fever which flows
But doesn't burn.
Rindles through the arteries of the mind.
The beauty of diseasedness.
For a near shore and distant pines,
Writhing in the mad magic
Of love and pain.

Time rusts in its
Idiocy and stupor,
Tearing rumpled make-up
Off the mirror.
Age stands by
The vestibules,
And the props lie
Heathen on the hearse,
A scarf, macabre and brown.

These roads are her smiles
Of a heart which knows no end.
Fogs of shimmering voices
And at the ridge to find her lonely, singing.
Or perhaps the inebriation
Running through the corridors
Of diffusions and delusions.
It is the silhouette.
She walks out in silent effigies—
Mortal, immortal—
Of a story which remains
Untold forever.

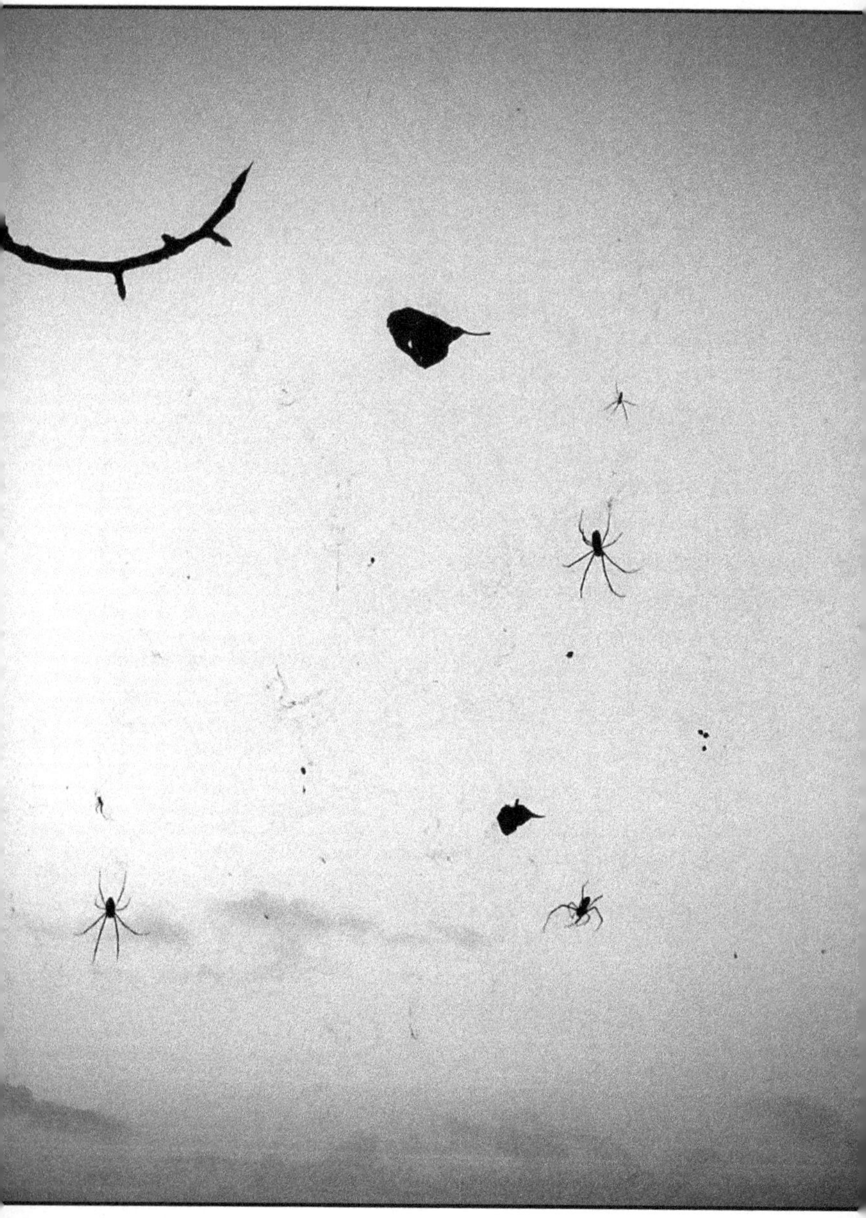

Kiarostami, The Sun and The Moon

Under a turquoise sky
A house is awake
Wee hours of night
The lamp burns at the window.

This house looks exactly the same
As other houses in neighbourhood
But someone is dying there
And the lamp burns at the window.

Seems there are mountains
Rivers and other lives
Seems there are cars, sunglasses
And schools
But the lamp burns at the window.

One day all the houses will merge
Into many doors
Steps and doors to other houses and sky
All walk towards an obscurity
There are no scripts for death
Let the pollens just fly in the air
The lamp should burn at the window.

Go River, I Wait

Looking at the weir,
the birth changes.

I fall like moonlight
on moored boats,
your shoulders.
Body's but a chalice.
Pour me in abundance,
tumbled and spilled.
I flow to
the core of your scent.

River floors,
a green darkness,
some sailors holding a lantern
knock at the door.

You join
your spread knees.
The ivy descends from
the hearth
in a sonata of silences.

Fire is far away.
Fire is far away.

Dive
in my cycle of

existence.
The sky tells anecdotes.

I will burn you
in the karmic light
of repugnance
to reincarnate in me
as my eyes,
my hands, maybe
my fingers,
so that you are inside my sight,
my touch, my flowers,
and my melancholy.

It is a shower of light
which gushesfrom under the water.
The chakras erupt,
and I enter the tree with you,
a seventh Destiny

in love and mirth,
in blood and semen,
in prayers and miracles,
in heresy and forgiveness,

in every atom of a day
and every gluon of a night.

Burning, She Melts

On a floor in a high-rise city,
Gnawing sounds of vehicles,
Deafening.
I let the burning cigarette's end touch between the fingers—
Arranged pain, yet sudden.
Long sighsbend the night sky.
The moon hides,
But the stars stay, wet and in dilemma of a twinkle.

Rooms, kitchen, bookshelves, chairs, corridors.
Walk past
Long yards of insecurity,
Carnal deviations,
Oblique shadows of the lamppost through French windows
Does the grandfather clock strike
Twelve—midnight?
No,
No one keyed it. My father, me, mom—
all went behind the clock
And ticked, listened to the gongs.

Lips I touch,
My body—a gun in a shower,
Programmed for various fornications,
Destinies, and classrooms.

Sometimes outside the classrooms,
In punishments and guilt,
Peeing in bludgeoned hallucinations.
Wooden boxes and curses
Stacked carefully
In stationaries beer mugs, pills, hollows,
And a premonition of a coming, what?

The balcony, always a final step
From a high floor.
Waters freeze in the body.
Spit first and see the spit fall down, down, and further down.
That will be you,
Rootless
While falling, mindless
And fateless
Throughout.
Nothing exists and has ever been created.
Emptiness is all.
All.

Mists, Jerks, and War on the Radio

Oblong shadows of longing.
Unmoved in the salon chair,
The coiffeur shaves all hair
Of love and caresses.
Waiting.

Addiction, is it not?
Of the poison.
Pain is a quick orgasm.
Sometimes blood,
Tears, or semen.

Night, at the call of wisps,
Descends, streaks of red cloud.
Lips touch.
Hedonistic pillows,
Calling you at the dungeon.
Feathers of moonlight.

The window grows
To usher in brims of rainbow,
Asks for a handful of dry leaves.
When your canvas burns
Of gluttony, hell has a decent climb
Of stairs.
Mystic corridor.

Arid eyes stare
From the stupor of death.
The search never ends.
Drowning in the ceiling
Of friendship, treacherous
Frames.

Left wallet and mellowed songs
From the radio, antique Buddha,
Orange walls of desires.
Which part of the body was it?
Only finger and fingernail.
A luminous letter whispers
Serpentine songs.

Ruhaniyat

The dervishes move, and the eclipsed moon
Fragrances splutter in the night sky.
Streaks of white clouds stare
Where our hands meet and grasp our souls.
The obelisk looms over a thought,
Its mysterious lips ripple through our faces.
Music enters the body,
Clots in pain, murders, and blood whizzes.
The carnival flows in blood, everything smothered.

The dervishes move,
Slowly changing the lights
Into a hue of colours, ecstasy, love.
And the castle collapses in darkness,
Uncanny windows green with jealousy, desires.
The garden stretches to royal eternities and mist,
And I take the path through the willows.
A eucalyptus rises, stretching her branches to you.
A boat still languishes on purple waves.
The pitch of a siren pierces the body;
I am deafened, cannot hear your voice any more.
Are you calling the mountains from your exile

The dervishes move, as if in dreams,
Not touching the ground, a dance so serenely haunting.
O melancholy, put a knife through my eyes and let me
fly high with them.

Mandala and the Soul

Moribund verses, cruel caricatures,
And I am in love, piquant wishes!
Burn like seven candles, deathly hallows,
Menstrual blood in spirited perfumes;
All in drinking ale—lick the taste of my thighs.

Gorgeous murder throbs in slimy nights.
Pavements made of skull bones,
Where a mystic walk douse the stars,
Dust of melancholy and spider's
Web, the hooting of a distant ship—
Go to the fluorescent water.
Nearness is not an arbitrary fruit.

Hush your breath; are you not dead?
The dotted sky stains from the patches of semen.
The allegory dances in the bends of a rainbow.
A mask is a mandatory habiliment,
And you have scorched your face in tenderness;
Hold each other and join.
True are the roots because
You have become a tree now.

Murmur.

The Bombing Starts When We Fuck

Strange roads in me.
Meandering through towns
With broken houses,
Stooping buildings,
Crashed cars,
Burning mausoleums,
Tilting banners,
Deserted markets,
Half-eaten dead bodies,
And some tanks and wagons
Wheezing past.
They have somewhere to go
Quickly.
The sky is stark in the sun.
Etched and fierce corners
Glazing over all
The debris,
Making them look
Explicit and crude.
Two steps further down, a hospital.
Beds heaped with children.
All with breathing masks.
All the eyes, open,
Yet not looking.
Some with scars.
For some, you don't see
Where the scars lie.

I run, gasping for breath.
Hills, clouded meadows.
Hills, hairpin bends.
And then suddenly the path
Turns into a ropeway,
Takes me over, through forests
And in between deep lakes
Like eyes of an emu,
Whose surfaces become like screens.
And I see from my cable car
Visions of unrest,
Of curfews, of mass killing,
Of rape and plunder,
And where the lakes end,
Through the forest, an enormous
Black hand runs, like a cheetah,
Scraping off the trees,
Upturning the earth, for minerals,
For more roads, for oils,
For riches, for more, for more.

Near here, the ropeway ends.
I land in a cottage of old men
Who do not talk in words,
Only whistles.
And the others understand.
They sit by the evening fire
And watch birds.
Sometimes a brown bear comes
Out of the jungle
To give them honey
And bulbs of plants,
Berries, and pine seeds.
They all dine together.
They all.

From Nowhere, Sulking

Distances roll like waves, coming near, going far away, sometimes turbulent and then silent, much like Turner's ships. I have plotted distances in bed, between the linen sheets, between the pillows, between the inch of air between our little toes, which could have touched but are now a feather apart, apart like our minds, tearing, bruising, tormenting just to implode into each of ourselves.

Plotted distances bloom like sad azaleas, pinkish in their fading air. You sit around those, apparently underneath a tree which has no leaves but blooms to only flowers in the next spring. You sit and knit in the melting twilight, maladies for me, and after a time's knitting, you hold it up to see whether an imaginary me can flow into those, your knittings, and touch the lazy hours' caresses of the fingers.

Someone else is always a dear thought. Distances love these. Someone else watching movies with you, reading a book to you, and you have spoken words to him which remind you of me. Someone else starts looking like me in these distances, perhaps the shoulder, maybe the hands, or the way my lips twitch in smiles, the light which reflects on my lips, making it blackishly red. You smell me when you touch his hands; you feel me when you lift those to your face. And perhaps kiss.

Distances thirst for kisses. The other night, I choked with a thirst for a kiss. I pouted, raised my lips to kiss, moistened my lips with my tongue, bit them; but the thirst engulfed the lips, the eyes, the throat, the mind. And then I went to the bathroom to wash off my lips, my eyes, my face—wash it off to the drains, to the canals. Today, in the morning, they said my lips were still floating around the River Kennet, around the dark turns, and my eyes under the pass where the old church is.

Here fire gives smoke and smoke alarms. Many said that when they forget to turn off the cooking hob, the smoke comes, and the alarm sets out. Then everybody has to obey the alarm, come out of their rooms, move in lines, go out in the cold, march in queues, and again follow the alarm to enter the building. I want to do that, obey the alarm. But here it does not ring. I have the fire, I have the smoke, and I have all the devastations; but the alarm does not ring, does not ring. Distances enter the alarm, spread roots, choke them, and destroy the machine, so I don't know when a fire becomes a smoke. A smoke becomes a snake, and the snake bites my tongue, bites my ears, bites my memories, and gorges me down the path of a black alley, where I float forever, for distances, for a ship which has lost its way in the mist of timelessness.

The Far, The Sadness

Footsteps embalmed on the sand, gradually disappearing into the far pines; the dusk calling; silence; the sudden roars of the waves, tottering, moaning, telling something to the ripe and dark clouds; phosphorus; and a broken boat of sadness—that's the sea. I am to sit here under the "moonness", trying to empty my mind of hunger, lust, and the corrugated tricks and trite of my mundanity. See the sudden and silent flight of some unknown flock of birds high up against a vague sky where there is no light, no darkness, not a single star nor a void, nor a mind which seeks the shape or colour of everything. Let it ripple. Let it whisper. Let it fall off and flow away. If you have not touched it, if you have not felt it, then it would be the other life which shadowed, embraced, and then walked down one day, barefoot, the way of the sand, to the pines, and only left footsteps in the dusk, silence, and the sudden roars of the waves. Can you hear?

She Was, Who Is

The fire has come too close,
Now melting her lips and eyes.
The fire has come too close,
Cracking her jaws and skull.
Yesterday she was in AC.
Yesterday she felt very hot.
Yesterday the nurse gave her a newspaper.
Yesterday she wanted to listen to *Madama Butterfly*
And cry—she had her eyes then.

Howling that night, the thunderstorm;
She called her life a revolt.
Smashed so many glasses and nights,
Rotten hearts, brilliantly swaying her cape
And rising to the sun.
A firework which darkness could give.
A firework which people bent their necks to see.
The embellishment of pain:
Her love, her trust, the desertions.
Dipped the fingers in her breasts
And blood she wrote.
Blood she wrote.

Tomorrow her linen needs to be changed.
Tomorrow her insulin stock gets over.
The writing pad at its last, if she
Suddenly asks for a scribble.
Tomorrow her ashtray needs a clean.
Tomorrow, in the middle of night, will she wake?
Late, not returning to bed, crying hiccups in the dark.
Or in a violent shiver, trying to gasp for breath,
Breathe a 'Hold me, hold me', she will
Tomorrow.
Tomorrow, will she?

Darkness, tilting. Dreams, through a nightness. I see an earth floating in the cosmos and a serpent coiling around it, the body of the serpent luminous and evil, with three hideous heads and venomous sets of eyes. It looks at me and drips venom; drops fall to a violet ocean, where a child's dead body floats, as if in peaceful sleep, drifting towards the dark shore, where other similar bodies are heaped under a giant clock, say, of the railway station. I run out of the station and step into a jungle of words, thorns, weeds, and sentences. I spell a word, and a thousand meanings clog, making a maze. I search and search, while five hands come out of my body, each one with a smartphone in it. I relentlessly key in with my fingers, and new mes are born—in millions. They group to become the *devatas* and *rakshasas*, and they start scouring the ocean in search of the amrit, the nectar—more money, power, and sovereignty. But the amrit never comes, and everything uprooted gets consumed, killed, and devastated: memories, love, hope, bliss, beauty. But the search continues on and on and on.

Deep Scratches Lick My Heart

Some letters flawed, ragged Philomela
Lies obtuse on the violated ink, grey in the sullied blankness
Muddled vision and the nightingale
A flight in a silent garden, choked voices
A larder of memories floats on the paper
Oozes vile blood: my face, eyes, and lips.

Dead leaves talking in the surreal graveyard
Don't let the phoenix rise
Ashes buried under the asphalt of the city, darkness
Looking at the torso of the old woman
Climbs up the stairs with a blue lamp trembling in her hands
The flames quiver, the night
Distant trotting of the horses and shrill sirens of ships
Dried harbour, melancholy, and wisps of a ghostly smell.

I stand waiting for the recluse light
under the weeping mulberry
Lift me to my disappearance from things around
The trunk of the rhino dazzling and the burnt face of a ferocious monkey
Cold sounds of water and wickers floating
Tossing through the stones
I trust the water, I trust the water
Leaves and thorns where I come back
My unknown sojourn, where do I come back from?

The snake moves, leaving her second skin
Back in my yards, coil through the grouchy roots
My coffin travels below, six feet under
And under the ruins of a city, houses
Hallways, windows, baths, and mazes of debris
Frozen dead, with an ancient haze of eyes
All float in brilliant passages, bleak red
To the core of the earth,
For erupting again and again and again.

Jumping to The Next Cosmos

Thoughts: vivid blue eyes and the repugnance of dreams
I kill the clouds
Dripping blood on the meadows, where the pine sprouts
And Neanderthal faces rise again—sulking and wise, again
I say to the old faces, 'Hey ho, look at me, I reign the world now, you stupid fools!'
Faces disappear, and the henge crushes my body
The parrot flutters away with a shrill shriek.

The red book never finishes
However much I read, tear off the pages, and still
Putting fingers in my daughter's mouth
Sinful wastes, she eats, laughing
I roll the globe around her feet
TV shows: she watches, undistracted
I set fire to her little home, walls, furniture, clothes, and the little everything
TV shows: she continues.

Sometimes it snows; the bone shivers, and the water goes through the veins, slithering, cold
Filling up forms—name, age, sex, address 1, address 2—I don't have a single one
Cities change, landscapes, the sky, but
The sameness of people

The skirmishes, morning walks, parties
Running in my head, heads—I have
to vomit—people, time, talks
A dead table of stillness, I know I lie there, frozen
Pushing till the end of the corridor, further and further
A hint of divine, darkness—who takes me?
Is it truth which can only exist in vagueness?

Night Rooms in London

Lights go off.
Yet it is not dark.
An imbecile shadow remains,
A shout of vividness:
I cannot love you in light.
Fearing your breasts, full of torture,
And your eyes, dull.
Not as in darkness, when
They become a river.

Light, sounds of light
Penetrate us, our nakedness,
Blemishes, bodies of imperfections.
My hands so full of sadness,
As if dead at the touch of your skin.
I coil, pull bed sheets on us.
Amber autumn leaves,
The depth of a cantata,
Frizz of the morning snow,
And glows of our nearness.

Yet
The holocaust remained.
The alertness.
Moist chambers of cruelty and intentions.
I erupt, you melt,
As in the order of things.

But nothing flowed.
The juice of obscureness,
Nectar of Horus.
The bird of togetherness
Fluttered in starkness,
Caged,
Feathers torn and stuck to the
Rinds of time, and finally died
In the flashing lights of a billboard,
Bloodless and blank.

The Canal

Walk along with me, beside the canal.
The path gradually becomes narrower,
With bursts of wild raspberries and weigela.
Sometimes the path drifts away from the water.
Only you can hear the cold sounds of the stream.
Some lonely houses line the other side of the shore.
Nobody seems to live in those houses.
And after a few yards, a thick growth of trees,
Many fallen trees (I don't know who cuts them),
And a wooden bridge with a board of caution:
'Beware, strong undercurrent'.
At times, white horses come galloping by the path.
We have to give way.
Random dead bodies on a stretcher,
Like the way they are carried for burning.
Also passing by are strange babies with the heads of dogs,
Buckled and sweetly strolled by their mothers.
The canal, beside it float a small lake and houseboats.
These pass silently over water,
Some with standing mercenaries having stiff faces,
And some with heaps of cannabis and other weed.
A few boats have only old couples.
Going in search of the setting sun,

They glide calmly with joined hands.
Walking thus, the evening descends.
The canal broadens and falls into the river, near a red dam.
Let us halt here; no more path there is.
Taking out from our sack the dried autumn leaves,
The little cans of sky,
The pills which will not let us talk,
And the flying wings.
There is further to go.
There is further to go.

Pieces and How I Am Becoming Lonely

This is my border.
Ordained on the sides by lush green meadows
And mountains.
Small brooks make their way through.
Little cottages
And bougainvillea.
Farm animals straying and munching.
Sometimes the line of entries go through
Serene villages and towns,
Silent backyards of people's homes.

This is my border.
Through rough lands
The barbed wire runs,
Of galvanised steel.
The turnbuckles and the hook-and-eye ropes,
All of super-strength.
Dumps of wire stocks.
Though at places, the wooden fence posts tumble,
The wire stretches taut and tensed.
No chance of trespassing.
Last winter, we returned
Eight hundred refugees
To our neighbours.

This is my border.
Towards the east where the jungle starts,
A set-up of watchtowers,
Barricaded and fortified.
The barbed wire electrocuted, foolproof.
In places, the fence shows traces of
Broken animal hands, legs,
Fur stuck between the rusted turns.
This spring, a mob of people got
Electrified, and a few bodies started burning
While trying to break through.
Finally, it rained, and the bodies were
Buried there, some alive.
It was about that time
When the enemy headquarters
Spread the news that we were trying to export drugs,
Stuffed in a baby's body, surgically hollowed out.
All silly and gossip.
The real charm is the
Main port of entry,
Shows artistically designed hoardings saying
'Bienvenida', 'Willkommen', 'Valkommen', etc.
It's claimed that we covered all 6,500
languages of the world.
This is my border.

In the Rugs of a Sufi

Keep me in your mystique,
Mellowed clouds!
And give me a willow on my way home,
When the evening sun
Blazes the golden dry leaves at her feet
To eternalise the facade of pain.

The shrill sound of wishes travels seas
To touch your melancholy leaves,
Or be it the dithered branches,
I care not.
I hold the vessel of my palm
To your blinding shower of light.
Step in me.

Scarred, my letters are.
Don't you see?
The ragged Philomela lying obtuse
On the violated ink.
And my vile blood craves
To shoot up again and again
In diphtherial spasms of carnal entrenchments.

Darkness galore in meditation,
And deciduous thoughts lie refrigerated
Like tomatoes.
Deep in the freezer, my dead eyes
Pensive and fishy.
Cover me up with the sand,
Ephemeral conversations.
The snail crawls to the pine, salty winds.

La Mer, La Mer, La Mer.

Summer, Pledge Not to Dream

A thin road disappears in the bush
And the hint of a wooden bridge
Brings the regal summer like
A lion walking up to the hillock
To give his wake-up roar.

The dried branches sprout green
In their posthumous existence
And I die of inebriation
Still thirsting for a drop of snow
A little mist and a trail
For the soul mountain along the
River of Acheron.

Loneliness drifts and
Spreads over the surreal clouds
I have nothing but a deserted bus stop
The sycamore bushes wait in stillness
A chariot to come, embellished in scriptures and rolls
And leading the chariot
A man in a white robe
With hollowed eyes
Scooped and killed.

Ahreman captures the sun and
Time freezes, a blinding white light of death
The small Persian sculpture
Rises from its shamanic bed
Its body parts all disjointed, fragile
A two-headed vulture
Sits on its right hand
Looking at the deserts far stretched
Hundreds of cups
Placed near the saguaro bush
Blood flows from the cup
A cave with demonic screams from inside
A cave with a thousand black suns.

A Cup of Time

Expressions.
Children's writing on the wall. Drawings of the house,
mountains, and paths. Scribbled rivers.
Oblique, amorphous spaces. The sun.
Windows open to a gigantic book.
Snowflakes covering the letters, words,
Especially where it says *mercy* or *love*.
Vivaldi dances in ecstasy on the vinyl,
Playing the pizzicato, winters mostly.
While spring arrives in the other room,
Elaborate flowers growing around your vulva,
Rivers through the golden thighs,
A velvet robe thrown to cover your nakedness.
Beauty tires.
With every bite of the apple,
My penis is growing but doesn't stand erect.
A blue pendulum hangs in the middle of the stage.
It tick-tocks between two words on either side,
Flesh and *wisdom*,
Uniformly swaying.
A marching at the backstage,
Dragging dead bodies to the pit.
Jesus looks at the red sky and
Declares more war.
Several clocks fall from emptiness,
As in Dali's painting,
Each with a different time,

And my father runs amok to
Key them, keeping the time,
Keeping the time.
And one day, the comet crashes on the road.
A long-planned crash—one in a million years.
Suddenly, the earth starts shrinking.
Everything come so close, closer.
Roads, houses, shadows, rooms, beds, relations,
You, me, our fakeness.
We implode and stand in a cosmic bathroom,
Floating through galaxies and stars.
A rendezvous.

Undress and
Come into the shower, touch me.
Let them see us naked.
The birds and the supernovas.

Movies and Graves of Kings

Trepidations of forsaken nights and gagged calls. The tap drips in the bathtub, and shadows of slimy hyenas devouring my thoughts. I wreck in pain, cross my arms and lie down methodically on the bed, frozen, timelessly.

The voice in the phone, on the other side, it's still me. Sometimes like a dead child floating over the sea, the voice is calm and morbid, with the shrill shrieks of seagulls and the breaking of waves, but no other sound. Who am I calling?

It is the story of a king who burnt the city in his reign and shut himself in a blazing room to read the works of his dearest poet. He read and read until the fire engulfed, scorched, and muted his voice.

Such is my corpse. With a lingering song on the burnt lips and floating on a boat on the dancing white waves, struck with moonlight and the lamenting shores, always distant, in a cry, calling with silent tears.

Strange noises, how they spread into branches, other trees. A picnic in the night with a lesser fire, enough to char the thighs and navel; the moony eyes caught between the twigs and charcoals need a stoking. Then all come in a delicious dish of an exotic gourmet. Pour the tangy sauce on the plate, garnish with red saffron, and sprinkle some unknown herbs. I am ready to be yours. Maud and meaningless.

About The Author

Anindya's camaraderie with words began from his childhood. With early exposure to world and Indian literature, he kept gadding about the fascinating alleys of prose, poetry, fiction, and non-fiction. Born in the cultural capital of India, Kolkata, Anindya's first tryst with the verse-makers were the oriental bards of poetry – namely Rabindranath Tagore, Jibanananda Das, Shakti Chattopdhayay, Sunil Gangopadhyay among others. The horizon widened with the works of Mirza Ghalib, Faiz, Rilke, Yeats, Wordsworth, Walt Whitman, Japanese Haiku masters, and many more magicians of the meter. From a tender age, Anindya found his voice through his poetic expressions, a passion which only grew deeper with time.

Anindya currently resides in the Southern Indian City of Bangalore and is employed as a management professional in a multinational corporation. 'Nothing Takes it All' is the first venture of Anindya to reach out and share his verses with a coterie of readers in the wider circle. These verses are sedimentation of the ramblings of his inner mind – evoked, disturbed, intrigued by the kerfuffle of the modern world. Above all, this book is an encomium celebrating the art form of poetry.

CPSIA information can be obtained
at www.ICGtesting.com
Printed in the USA
LVHW041623060123
736479LV00001B/141

9 781543 708929